TABLE OF CONTENTS

DESIGNER'S INTRODUCTION ....

MAKING THE MOLDS ....

BUILDING THE STEM ....

BUILDING THE TRANSOM 13

MAKING THE CENTERBOARD TRUNK 16

SETTING UP 18

BENDING THE FRAMES 20

ATTACHING THE FLOOR TIMBERS 21

THE FINAL SETUP 23

INSTALLING THE KEEL 24

PLANKING THE HULL 29

MAKING AND FITTING THE SHEERSTRAKE.....................................31

SMOOTHING, CAULKING, AND PAINTING 35

TURNOVER 37

THE SHEER CLAMPS 37

SOME DETAILS 40

BEAMS AND BULKHEADS 41

AFTER DECKING 44

COAMINGS, FOREDECK, AND COVERING BOARDS.............................45

BALLAST KEEL AND DEADWOOD 49

THE CENTERBOARD 51

THE RUDDER...51

THE SPARS AND RIGGING 52

AS-BUILT DETAILS 53

USE AND CARE 54

TABLE OF PLANK WIDTHS 56

SCHEDULE OF MAJOR FASTENINGS...57

NOTE: The instructions in this book require the use of complete construction plans, which are available from WoodenBoat Plans. For information on purchasing these plans, please see the inside back cover.

Cover illustration by Kathy Bray

Copyright © 1987
by WoodenBoat Publications, Inc.

Published by Woodenboat Publications
Brooklin, Maine 04616

Library of Congress Cataloging–in–Publication Data

Bray, Maynard.
    How to build the Haven 12½-footer.

    1. Sailboats. 2. Boatbuilding. I. Title.
VM351.B716 1987 623.8'223 87-23011
ISBN 0-937822-13-2

How to Build the
Haven 12 ½-Footer

DESIGNER'S INTRODUCTION

While the plans for the Haven 12½-footer say "designed by Joel White," and it is true that I did draw the plans, the concept and detailing of this design were developed by Nathanael Herreshoff back in 1914. His design, generally known as the Herreshoff 12½-footer or Buzzards Bay 12½-footer, produced the most popular of all Herreshoff-built boats, over 400 having been built by the Herreshoff Mfg. Co. A great many of these wonderful boats are still in existence, much beloved by their owners. All that I have done is to take the original 12½ and slightly modify the lines to reduce the draft by a foot, and to provide a centerboard to offset the loss of lateral plane. Our goal while drawing the plans was to secure a shallower hull without losing the essence of N.G. Herreshoff's original design, and without creating any noticeable change in performance. Toward that end, the displacement and stability of the two boats are identical, the fore-and-aft center of buoyancy is the same, and the same sail plans are used. The outboard profile above the water is also identical. In order to retain the same displacement and stability, the beam was increased some 3" amidships and 1½" at the stern. Although perforce the measurements are different and the sections were much altered below the waterline to reduce the draft, every possible attempt was made to reproduce the character of the body plan.

I had hoped that the new boat would closely resemble the old 12½s, and to this extent, I think we succeeded. If you see this boat on the mooring or out sailing from a vantage point that obscures the centerboard trunk, I don't think you can tell the new class from the old. What also pleases me is that the performance of the two classes seems to be exactly the same, both off the wind and to windward.

So let the credit for the excellence of these boats go where it is due—to the Wizard of Bristol, N.G. Herreshoff.

All this is leading up to an important point I want to make: not only was the 12½ design Herreshoff-inspired, but the Herreshoff construction method and the numerous exquisite details appearing in the original boats are much of the reason they lasted so long and have generated such affection in their owners. Maynard Bray and I have tried to illustrate these details and explain the construction at considerable length in order that future boats built to the Haven-class plans will also be long-lasting and well regarded by their owners.

The construction methods and the fine detailing are so much an integral part of the boats that to build one in a slapdash and crude manner is a sure invitation to disappointment in the finished product. Careful craftsmanship and attention to detail are required from the builder for the boat to equal the aesthetic and structural standards of the earlier Herreshoff boats.

—Joel White, N.A.

MAKING THE MOLDS

The Herreshoff Mfg. Co. method is what will be described for building this boat; that is to say, there will be a so-called timber mold for every one of the hull frames, and the hull itself will be built upside down. That means you'll be building some 22 individual timber molds (hereafter simply called molds), and while it is true that there are several faster ways to build a single boat—like using fewer molds and spanning between them with ribbands, for example—the method we'll be describing has significant advantages of its own. For one thing, the hull shape will be more faithful to the lines plan because there are so many more control points. And after a pair of frames (or timbers, as Herreshoff called them) has been steamed and bent around a mold, the unit can be conveniently positioned anywhere in the shop for fitting and attaching the floors, then set in its final location for planking the hull. The individual molds hold the frames in true transverse planes so bulkheads can be built snugly against them; and once you have invested in a set of molds for the first boat, reusing them to build subsequent hulls is very efficient. Meanwhile, the molds stack compactly for easy storage.

The molds will only take about three days to build, since the process is a repetitive one: the molds, although different from each other in size and shape, are nearly alike structurally. Although there are a number of ways to go about the mold-building process, I'll wager that the one used by Herreshoff (which is the one illustrated here) is about as good as you're apt to find. Although the first three photos show early stages of mold-building for the prototype boat, you'll start (with Step 3) by unrolling the full-sized mold pattern drawing and temporarily fastening it to your shop floor.

1 Lofting is not required, since the mold patterns and other furnished patterns have proven correct through building the first boat. If your molds match our patterns, you should have little, if any, fairing to do on them after they've been set up and aligned. (The edges of the molds will need beveling, however, as described later.)

The first boat did have to be lofted, however, and Photos 1–3 show how, from that lofting and the result-

ing "proven" offsets, the mold outlines were established through measurement. (Rather than using conventional height-and-half-breadth offsets, diagonal offsets were utilized, all of which radiated from a common point on the body plan's centerline—an approach occasionally used by N.G. Herreshoff. He claimed the advantages were obvious, and we found he was right. Not a single alteration was necessary for the 22 molds built to this offset table; after beveling, they all proved to be perfectly fair.

2 Nails were driven on each of the diagonals where the station mold crossed it, so the outer edge of a batten would lie along the offset markings. The batten was adjusted, if necessary, until it lay fair.

3 The line being marked here along the batten's edge is the same as that on your full-sized mold pattern drawing. Thus, as mentioned earlier, there is no need for you to perform Steps 1 and 2. You may find it convenient to use the following method, defined by Steps 3–27, in marking and building the molds. Start by nailing a flexible batten over the drawing, with its outer edge aligned with the appropriate mold outline.

The batten being used here is fiberglass, which can be bent to a tight curve without breaking. If you use wood, saw the battens from green (unseasoned) oak in two or three different thicknesses. (Obviously, there are other ways of marking the mold stock for cutting. Use the method that suits you best.)

4 The small finish nails that hold the batten in position have to be driven down so they're flush with the top edge of the batten; then you can lay the first piece of mold stock in position on the batten as shown, blocking underneath to hold it level. The mold stock shown here is two layers of common pine 1 x 10" (which dresses out to about ⅞ x 9½"). The layers are lightly nailed together and should be placed so their

ends overlap the construction baseline (at the right of the picture) and the diagonal line A-A shown on the mold pattern plan.

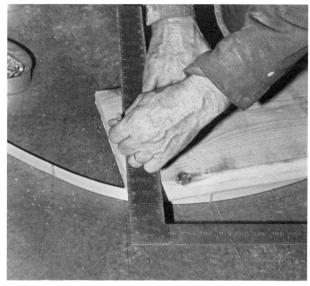

5 Now mark for the first cut by holding a straight-edge vertically aligned with the diagonal A-A.

6 Lay the next section of doubled mold stock so that its upper end overlaps the same diagonal, its lower end overlaps the vertical centerline at the keel, and its outboard edge just hangs out over the batten. Mark the end vertically above the diagonal.

7 Saw both sections of mold stock just outside the marked lines...

8 ...and plane them square and to the marked line...

9 ...checking for squareness, as shown.

10 Now draw the mold-section butts tightly together and hold them that way, using a draw dog made from a nail whose head has been sawn off and whose shank has been bent as shown. When driven into the wood, its outward spreading legs will pull the butts together and hold them that way while you mark them.

11 You'll need a wooden "clothespin" marker (sawn from a piece of solid stock) to transfer the curved shape of the batten along to the upper face of the mold stock (where it's convenient to use a pencil and see what you're doing). Using clothespin and pencil as shown, and with the butt blocked as necessary, mark along the mold from one end to the other (baseline to keel).

12 At this time, mark also for the cut at the construction baseline.

13 & 14 With the marking complete, the mold sections can be separated at the butt by removing the draw dog, then sawn out and planed square to the marked lines (outline and baseline butt). Keep the layers nailed together for now, however.

The batten has served its purpose and can be removed, allowing the mold sections to be laid into place directly on the mold pattern plan. With the baseline butt aligned with the construction baseline, bring the curved edge of the mold stock to its corresponding station line. Temporarily nail it there.

15 Now lay the next section in position against the first and nail it as well.

16 Mark for the cut at the vertical centerline over the keel as shown; saw and plane square to the line, as for the other butts.

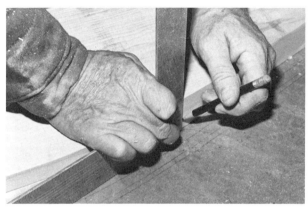

17 Transfer the sheerline from the mold pattern plan to the edge of the molds. This is a critical line; you'll be using it later, when the boat has been set up.

18 At this point, the so-called "station face" of the mold—the one that controls the shape of the boat at that point—has been cut to its final shape. The layers can be separated and the top one used for the other side of the boat. That side can be located by the sheer offset and the careful alignment of butts.

19 When the station face members of the mold are located to your satisfaction and temporarily nailed there, you can attach the cross spall, a length of 4" or 5" mold-thickness stock whose bottom edge (the edge facing the boat's keel) is positioned at the sheerline. That way, even if the penciled sheerline markings disappear, the edge of the cross spall always remains a dependable reference.

20 The mold pattern drawing gives a sheerline-to-top-of-keel distance, and this measurement sets the location of the lower edge of the lower tie-piece. Nail the piece temporarily.

21 You'll need another tie-piece at the bilge, and it, too, can be nailed for marking.

22 The "clothespin" comes into use again here to mark out the tie-piece.

23 You'll need two identical tie-pieces, and the easiest way to make them is to nail a second piece beneath the one you just marked and saw them both out together.

24 Screw the bilge ties in place as soon as they've been sawn out. There's no need to smooth up their edges, because, unlike the station face members, they'll not be used as references.

25 Saw out the lower tie-piece to shape, and screw it down.

26 The mounting brackets come next. These are of $1\frac{1}{2}$ x $1\frac{1}{2}$" lightweight steel angle, sawn to be about 2" wide and drilled as shown. They'll be bolted to the molds (the holes are being drilled in the photo) and, later on, lag-screwed to the shop floor. A wooden "angle iron" that the molds can be pushed against helps in locating the mounting brackets flush with the baseline.

27 Here are the molds ready for setting up. Notice that the first few are straight enough in their shape so they can be made with one piece, baseline to keel, and, as a result, can be of single thickness. The molds in way of the centerboard trunk have to be cut to allow the trunk to be set in place before the keel is installed or the hull is planked. There are a number of ways to provide a slot; I found it most convenient to build the molds all just alike, then modify them later for the centerboard trunk. Their construction is shown in later photos.

BUILDING THE STEM

28 After the oak stem stock has been planed to the required 1¾" thickness, you can transfer the shape of each of the pieces that make up the stem by means of carbon paper laid under the drawing and on top of the oak as shown.

29 Saw the pieces out on a bandsaw, then...

30 ...plane them to the line and square to the original face. Accuracy is especially important at the scarfs where the pieces will later join.

31 The flat surfaces of each scarf are best fitted first. You can see through the joint if the fit isn't good.

32 The end notches can be fitted by sawcutting after the faces are fitted. After clamping the stem pieces to each other, keep cutting and pushing them together until both notches are tight and to the line.

33 Check the overall exactness of the stem assembly by laying it over the pattern with the scarfs fitted together. Mark for the scarf bolts with a straight-edge, as shown. Also mark the station lines where they cross the stem; you'll use them when you set the boat up.

34 Bore for the ¹/₄" bolts while the pieces are clamped securely together. The vertical stick is an alignment guide for the drill.

35 Rather than using thick bedding compound, which is slippery and messy, I used red lead primer in the stem scarfs to seal the grain against the entrance of moisture.

36 The heads of the carriage bolts should be ground with two flats, as shown, so they won't interfere with later beveling of the stem to its face width. A ring of cotton wicking under the bolt head ensures that water can't leak past it, and the red lead primer being applied here will waterproof the cotton.

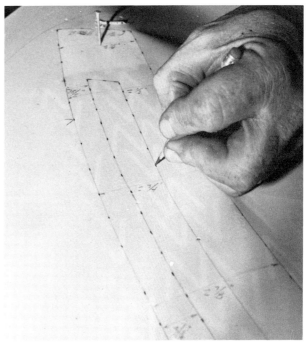

37 Marking for the stem's rabbet is the next operation, and this is done directly from the pattern, again using carbon paper. Make the marks close enough together so you can connect them by eye on the wood's surface after the pattern has been removed. Now is a good time to install the ⁵/₈"-diameter pine stopwaters, since it's easier to start their holes on an unrabbeted surface. Stopwater locations are shown on the drawing; they should center on the joints partway between the rabbet and middle lines where subsequent caulking will cross them.

38 As I begin cutting a rabbet, I find it easier to rough out a length of it by eye, then go back and work it down to the line at the correct angles. (Note: Don't cut the rabbet all the way to the heel of the stem at this time; instead, leave 8–10" uncut until the keel is bolted in place, after which the rabbet of the stem can be faired to that of the keel.)

39 A piece of plank-thickness stock ($\frac{1}{2}$" in this case) serves to guide the cutting process. The squared-off end of the stick should come just flush with the surface of the stem at the marked rabbet line, while the stick's inside surface should lie against the middle and bearding lines; the included angle within the rabbet should always be 90°.

40 A scraper helps in smoothing the rabbet after it has been chiseled out to the correct shape.

41 After the rabbets have been cut and smoothed on both sides of the stem, the stem face can be marked for beveling. Begin by drawing two lines $\frac{1}{2}$" apart ($\frac{1}{4}$" out from the centerline).

42 The stem face width increases toward the stemhead, as shown, so there will be space for the forestay chainplate. Mark for cutting with a batten, so as to mark two fair lines. The width at the top of the stem should be 1¼", as shown in the construction plan. The face width at the stem's heel should also grow so it can fair in with the taper of the keel. If in doubt, leave some extra wood; it's easy enough to grind it away after the stem/keel scarf has been bolted, but more difficult to add it back if you've cut away too much.

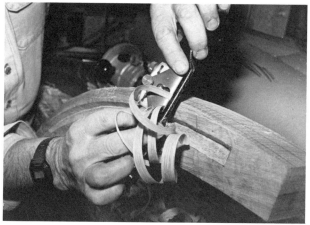

43 Use whatever tool is most natural to cut away the wood between the rabbet line and the stem face line, beveling the stem as shown.

44 The stern knee is marked and sawn out just as the pieces that made up the stem—in fact, I used the same stock and, after sawing it to shape, resawed it to the specified 1½" thickness on a table saw, as shown.

45 Because it is so much easier to work, I used fairly green oak for the stem assembly and stern knee; to keep it from checking, I gave them a good, thick coat of red lead primer before setting them aside for later use.

BUILDING THE TRANSOM

46 Begin by making full patterns for the transom's faces (inner and outer) of thin plywood, using the half-width paper patterns furnished. Then select some choice, dry stock 6" to 10" in width and plane in $\frac{1}{16}$" or so thicker than you want the finished transom to be—the extra thickness to allow for gluing misalignments ($\frac{15}{16}$" is about right for this $\frac{7}{8}$" transom). Cut the planks roughly to length according to the transom pattern, and carefully joint the mating edges straight and square so the pieces lie wood-to-wood with no seams open.

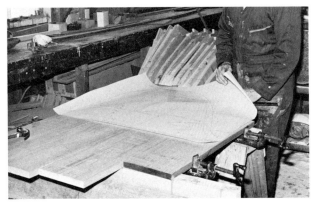

47 Check that all is well by clamping the jointed pieces together and placing the pattern over all. (You'll be using the plywood pattern made in Step 46 rather than the Mylar one shown here.) This is the time to decide where you want the bronze drifts to be located so they'll do their job without interfering with the tiller port, the rudder gudgeon, or any of the transom's finished edges. Just where the drifts should go depends partly on where the seams fall, and this is generally different for each transom. Drifts strengthen the transom against splitting, and I find it is best if they are laid out to pass through two transom planks and go partway into a third; that way, they're long enough to do some good, yet not so long that they can't be bored for and driven fairly easily.

48 This is the drift pattern for this particular transom, the drift locations, their lengths and ending points marked on the clamped-together transom stock. The drifts were cut from $\frac{1}{4}$" bronze rod.

49 A guide helps ensure that each drift hole is started exactly halfway through the thickness. A stick (not shown) should be clamped as previously shown for the stem scarf so that the hole stays centered and follows the drift's marked line. For drifts that go all the way through, start drilling from carefully marked locations on each edge so the holes meet in the middle of the plank, where misalignment won't affect the plank-to-plank fit. Make sure that the holes are a little deeper than you need so there will be no danger of the drift bottoming out before the joint closes. Check that there is a good match between drill and drift in a piece of scrap before you begin on the transom itself. There should be a light-drive fit, with a hammer setting the drift about 1" deeper in the hole with each blow.

50 Start by fastening the second piece onto the top one after the joining wood edges have been spread with epoxy glue. Drifts help hold the desired alignment at this stage as well as guard against splitting later. The leading ends of the drifts don't need to be pointed like a nail, but they should be rounded a bit to eliminate sharp corners so they'll drive easier and not enlarge the hole by tearing away wood while being driven. Follow this same process for each piece of the transom, and clamp the whole unit together with bar clamps.

51 After the bar clamps have been taken up fairly snugly, wipe off the excess glue, lay the assembly on plastic-covered bearers that have been checked for a twist-free alignment, and clamp it down. Then you can take up on the bar clamps pretty much without fear of the thing going out of line. However, before you walk away, it pays to check with a staightedge that there's no built-in warp. Just a little care now can save you loads of time later on.

52 After the glue has cured and the clamps have been removed, the excess glue should be scraped away so that the pattern will lie flat upon the surfaces. Pick the best side of the glued-up panel to be the outside face; this is especially important if the transom is to be varnished later. You can sand and seal the two faces at this time if you wish. The combined scraping, sanding, and perhaps some planing should remove the $\frac{1}{16}$" additional thickness and result in a transom panel that measures about $\frac{7}{8}$". Precision is not too critical here, but keep in mind that the transom patterns are based on a $\frac{7}{8}$" thickness and the edge bevel those two outlines represent will be slightly inaccurate if your transom is thicker or thinner than designed.

53 Using the plywood pattern for the transom's inside (larger) face—the one you made in Step 46—mark the transom outline for cutting. (Mylar is being used here, but a full wooden pattern is better, I think.)

54 Using the transom bevels shown on the drawing as a guide, saw out the transom outline. The bevel is extreme under the turn of the bilge— more than the 45° limit for most saws— so saw what you can...

55 ...and plane the rest, always checking with a bevel gauge at the appropriate locations. As with the lower part of the stem face bevel, it will be better to delay planing the final transom bevel until after the boat has been set up, at which time you'll find the plywood outside-face pattern (made in Step 46) useful. All you have to do at this point is get the transom cut down to the outline of its inner face and get rid of most of the bevel wood.

MAKING THE CENTERBOARD TRUNK

56 Two ³/₄" plywood sides, a pair of rabbeted oak bedlogs, and three uprights (sometimes called posts, standards, or end pieces) also of oak make up the centerboard trunk. The shapes for all are included in the plans package; it's simply a matter of transferring these shapes to the wood and cutting to the lines. There is a sequence of assembly that will make the job easier. First, however, clamp the mating posts to one of the sides, check that they fit as they should, and drill for the screws. Do the same for the bedlogs (both side pieces, both bedlogs); then take the whole thing apart, blow off the drill shavings, and you're ready for final assembly.

57 Coat one of the sides, where the posts will lie, with 3M 5200, as shown.

58 The posts can now be permanently attached to that side piece.

59 Coat the faying surfaces of the bedlog with 3M 5200...

60 ...lay the sidepiece in the rabbet...

61 ...clamp it where it belongs, and screw the side piece to it. Do the same thing for the other side-piece/bedlog assembly.

62 The two assemblies can now be clamped together and drilled. Make sure that the undersides of the bedlogs are aligned by using a framing square, as shown in Photo #64.

63 Before final assembly, it's a good idea to give the exposed inner surfaces a coat of antifouling paint, since they'll be hard to get to afterwards. And don't forget to smear on enough 3M 5200 to keep the unit from leaking.

64 Make a final check that the undersides of the two bedlogs line up with each other, by using a framing square and a block of correct thickness, as shown. Then tighten the clamps to draw the two sides together.

65 After the screws are all driven and the squeezed-out 3M 5200 has been wiped off, the bedlogs should be sawn flush with the ends of the trunk, as shown here, and bolted to each other through the posts, as shown on the drawings.

66 Cut off the tops of the posts as well, and, if necessary, plane the trunk's edges so they're square with the sides. Bung the screw heads, give the trunk's six vertical corners a "sandpaper round," and prime-coat the whole unit. At the bottom, the posts should project about 2". (They'll be trimmed to final length later when the keel is in place.)

67 Herreshoff boats are set up upside down on a construction baseline, and this line starts out as a top corner of a $^7/_8$ x $2^1/_2$" softwood backbone piece which runs from bow to stern, straight as you can make it. It doesn't have to be level, only straight—when viewed from above and from the side. Closely spaced shingles act as shims at each of the fastening locations, and a long straightedge helps establish how much shimming is needed. After the backbone has been "installed" by temporarily screwing it to the shop floor, the boat's stations should be laid off on the backbone and numbered at $7^1/_2$" intervals.

68 Each mold is to be set up on a pair of pads consisting of opposing wooden wedges which can be slid past each other to vary the height of the upper wedge's top surface. The first step is to locate the pads on the shop floor by squaring out from the

station line marked on the backbone in the preceding step. Distance out is figured by measuring the space between the mounting brackets on the mold you're about to set up, and dividing that space by two.

69 Now comes the leveling, accomplished as shown, to bring the pad surface to the same height as the backbone at that station. When you've finished, the straightedge should just touch in three places (the two pads and the backbone) while the spirit level shows a centered bubble.

70 Steps 68 and 69 result in molds that are properly spaced, leveled, and squared horizontally with the construction baseline. What remains is to square them vertically with the baseline. (If that line happens to be horizontal, the mold faces will be vertical, but that isn't at all necessary with this setup.) Use the big wooden square shown in Photo 68, laying it vertically against the face of the 'midship mold and the backbone piece. Then run opposing diagonal braces (one pair forward and another pair aft) from the 'midship mold to the shop floor, making certain, of course, that the mold is aligned squarely before the braces are fastened. (One pair of diagonal braces shows in this photo, which was taken somewhat later in the construction process.) With the 'midship mold as a secure and reliable reference, all other molds can be properly spaced and then connected to it by means of light battens shown here and in subsequent photos.

71 On a small boat like this, it's possible to bevel the molds and have the square-section frames lie along their beveled edges. (Larger boats built by Herreshoff used heavier frames that were too stiff to conform to beveled molds, and the outboard face of each frame had to be beveled for every new boat.) Thus, the next operation after setting up the molds is beveling them so that a batten will bear along the entire edge rather than hitting a high corner. For this boat, I sawed some of the bevel into the molds as I built them, but I wouldn't bother with this cumbersome operation again, because it's so easy to do the rough-beveling with a power grinder.

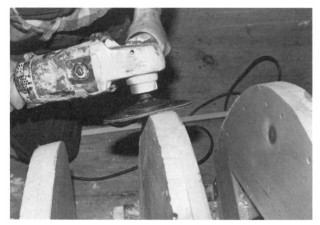

72 By eye, you can estimate the correct bevel and grind away the unwanted wood—but be careful, and make sure that the station-face corner of the mold is left untouched. (As mentioned earlier, this is the after corner of the molds forward of amidships and the forward corner of the after molds.) Use very coarse—No.16—discs, and wear eye and nose protection; you'll be making a lot of dust.

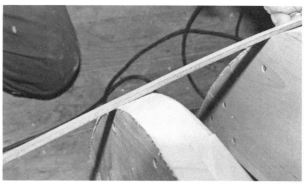

73 Check frequently with a batten to make sure you're not grinding away too much. The mold edge should look about as shown in the photo after rough-grinding; that is, there should be a little wood left for fine-tuning.

74 The spokeshave and block plane are good tools for fine-tuning the edge bevel on the molds. Let me repeat that the object is to have the batten lie fair and in full contact when placed anywhere on the set-up molds, and at the same time to not disturb the station-face corner of the molds. Use a felt-tipped pen to mark that corner if you wish.

75 Once you get the hang of beveling, the work goes fast; you should be able to complete all of the molds in a couple of days. Having three or four battens "at the ready" as shown gives a quick, convenient, and frequent means of checking the bevel as you work it down. Keep the molds connected together and more or less square with the backbone while you bevel them. Slight misalignment, I've found, doesn't hurt much at this stage, but don't overdo it.

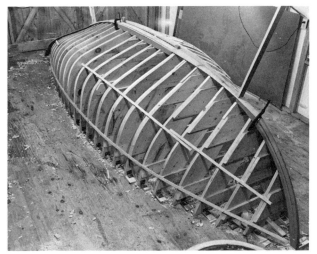

76 Here is a check of the complete setup, with the molds all beveled, the stem and transom mounted, the centerboard trunk in place, and the keel pattern sprung over all. (The transom mounting jig and the keel pattern measurements show on the drawings.) If things fit as they should now, you're ready for framing and planking. Notice how the sheer batten runs along in line with the corners of the cross spalls, just as it should, because you located those cross spalls at the sheerline earlier when you built the molds.

BENDING THE FRAMES

77 For the first boat, you'll now be taking apart all of your hard work so that the frames can be bent around the molds and have their floor timbers conveniently attached. (Subsequent hulls won't require this initial setting-up/mold-beveling operation.) Don't despair, however—the setup, once it's been proven, goes back together very easily. You'll also be sawing out the frames about now; they should be of unseasoned white oak and measure $^{13}/_{16}$" square after planing. Length varies, depending where they'll be used in the boat. The longest frame is about 54".

78 Flat staples made of light sheet metal have been fastened to the molds, as shown, to form a socket. The frames will need about an hour of steaming, after which one end is placed in the socket and wedged tightly to the mold, and the other end is bent around the curve of the mold as shown. Twist the frame as you bend it so it will lie snugly against the mold's beveled edge. You may need to drive a small nail here and there on the more steeply beveled molds to keep the frame from slipping "downhill."

79 Here is a close-up of the socket and wedge as they hold a frame end.

80 The hot frame can be temporarily clamped to the mold; sliding bar clamps work well here.

81 Draw dogs of a slightly different pattern come into play again here, replacing the bar clamps and holding the frame against the mold. Only two or three dogs will be needed per frame, and you'll find that they work better if the unflattened, hooked-over end is bent to more or less match the mold's bevel. The flattened, pointed end is bent a little less than 90° so the dog will draw in the frame when that point is driven into the mold. These are made from 30 D. common nails whose heads have been sawn off and whose shanks have been bent about as shown. Draw dogs are great little things—easy to make, compact, inexpensive, and very effective. Their angles can be adjusted at any time with a blow or two from a hammer.

82 Here is a pair of frames bent over a mold and held there by draw dogs. If a dog doesn't pull quite enough when you drive it into the mold, knock its hooked-over end sideways along the frame to tighten it, as has been done to the right-hand draw dog in the photo. Make sure you get the frame in full contact with the mold before it cools and stiffens.

83 This shows how the molds were modified so the centerboard trunk could be installed at an early stage.

ATTACHING FLOOR TIMBERS

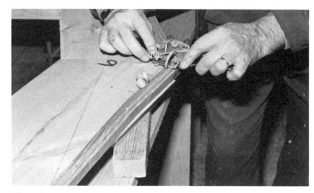

84 In most cases, the frames will have to be beveled a bit at their lower ends so the floor timbers can lie against them. Bevel outwards to just beyond where the floor-to-frame fastenings will be, or about two-thirds of the face width. A shim under this part of the frame pushes it above the surface of the mold so you can operate the spokeshave. Beveling can die out beyond where the top of the floor timber will lie.

85 This temporary cleat will index the floor-timber stock while it is being marked and is placed on a line representing the top edge of the floor timber. Measurements for locating the line appear on the mold pattern drawing.

86 The shapes of the floor timbers are arrived at by marking the appropriate face of each frame onto the oak floor-timber stock. Floor timbers are either $7/8$" or $1\frac{1}{8}$" thick, depending on where they go in the boat. The extra thickness is for the passage of ballast keel bolts, whose location is clearly shown on the drawing. Fairly seasoned oak is preferred for floor timbers so the keelbolts won't later loosen from wood shrinkage.

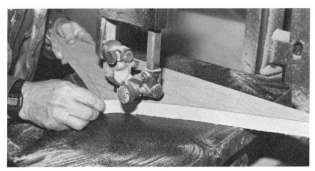

87 Each floor-timber arm is sawn to the same bevel as that of the corresponding mold. Floor-timber heels are cut to the bevels and measurements given on the mold pattern drawing. Rough sawing is OK for now; any smoothing can take place after setup.

88 A bevel board, made from information shown on the mold pattern plan, is a great convenience in sawing floor-timber heels.

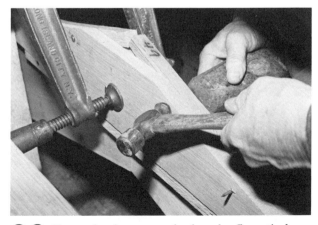

89 Frame heels are attached to the floor timbers, using three No. 10 copper rivets per crossing. Bore the holes a little undersize for a light-drive fit.

90 Projecting frame ends and molds can be sawn off to the line of each floor timber after riveting. The majority of the floor timbers are in one piece and placed to face amidships (see the construction drawing), but, as shown, there are some exceptions: the floor timbers alongside the centerboard trunk are in halves, and the one at the forward end of the trunk is placed facing away from amidships. All this shows in the drawings, but it is something to keep in mind when making the molds, attaching the floor timbers, and setting up the boat.

91 Except at the bulkhead (station number 7), the floor timbers need limber holes for the fore-and-aft drainage of bilgewater. The limbers can be sawn as shown and should be about ³/₄" wide and ¹/₂" deep, or the equivalent in cross-sectional area. Their location should be clear of where the keelbolts will be placed.

THE FINAL SETUP

92 After the frame assemblies have been completed, the molds can be set up on their pads again—an easy task, this second time, because you'll be using the same mounting bracket fastening holes (and, hopefully, a power screwdriver). The centerboard trunk is being dropped into place in the photo, an operation that is most easily done before all the molds are in place. The half-floors should be checked beforehand to make sure they'll all bear evenly on what will be the top surface of the bedlogs; the fit of the cut-off ends of these half-floors is less critical, since there is no fastening passing through in that direction. Note that the lower corners of the half-floors have been cut away to form limbers, and that the faying surfaces have been prime-painted with red lead. If you want to bore some 1" holes in a few of the floor timbers (like those in the floor nearest the camera), you'll be able to rig a rope lifting sling through them and haul and launch the boat the same way Herreshoff used to. These holes also act as additional limber openings when the bilgewater is above them.

93 The baseline-to-keel height at each end of the centerboard trunk should conform to that given on the mold pattern plan. The trunk can be shimmed from the molds, if necessary, to bring it where it should be.

94 There will probably be a little fairing and adjusting needed, now that the floor timbers and frames are riding on the molds. Keep shaving away until a batten shows a fair surface over which the planking will lie. Remember, however, that the planking will draw a low frame into being fair with those adjacent to it.

95 Having the hull upside down and at a convenient working height really begins to pay dividends now. Remember that the diagonally braced 'midship mold is what holds things square with the baseline and that connecting battens nailed to the frames as shown will be needed until the keel has been installed. Even after that, it's a good idea to use a few battens to hold spacing at the bilge, until the hull is about half planked.

96 The underside of the keel pattern made in Step 76 should have been marked with the correct location of each station line and, ideally, the station face of each mold should be brought to meet that line. There should then be 7½" spacing between the mold station faces—in theory, at least—and the keel pattern should lie fair on the floor timbers and bedlogs. Chances are that you'll have to do some compromising to achieve a fair structure for planking. When you've aligned the setup as well as you think possible (you may find that shimming a floor timber here and there helps), readjust the connecting battens to hold all the molds to the braced 'midship one.

INSTALLING THE KEEL

97 The keel timber, sawn from 1³⁄₈" oak to the shape of the pattern, has to be steamed to its curved shape. This is most easily accomplished right in place on the boat. First, of course, the keel must be fitted at the centerboard slot so it can slip over the posts there, and thus establish its fore-and-aft position. Bagging first one end of the keel for a couple of hours of steaming, then the other, worked well for us. Simply make a tube of some 6-mil poly film, staple it together (a little leakage won't hurt a thing), slip it over one end of the keel, stick a steam hose in it, and you're in business. Tie the ends of this plastic steaming tube closed to cut down on escaping steam. One of our tubes was so tight that it puffed up like a balloon after a few minutes; the other leaked and was less spectacular. But both did the job beautifully.

98 It's an easy bend, and not much force is required. A shore from the overhead helps bring the keel down against the floor timbers and stem.

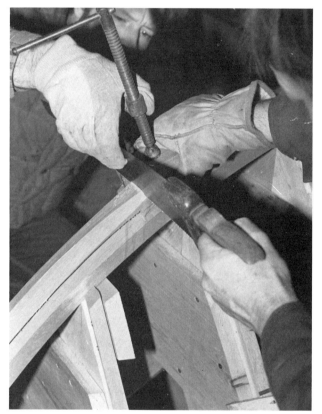

99 The keel's forward end has to lie tightly against the stem to form a scarf. Chances are that the butt of the scarf will need trimming before the keel can be drawn into position with C-clamps. This photo shows the butt being cut to length (sawing away wood from the stem with the saw guided by the end of the keel) as the first step in making the joint. Do this while the keel timber is still hot so it can be forced to conform to the flat of the stem scarf by clamping the two pieces together.

100 This is what the keel-to-stem joint should look like after fitting and before fastening. The lower part of the stem rabbet has been deliberately left uncut; it always pays to rabbet the keel and stem as a unit in this area to ensure a fair transition from one member to the other.

100a The after portion of the keel is bagged and steamed in the same way as forward. Its end can simply overhang the transom and be trimmed later. The keel should remain clamped to the bedlogs and held in its curved position atop the floor timbers for a few days so there will be minimum springback when you take it off for beveling.

101 Boring for the keelbolts comes next. Bolt sizes are listed on the drawing. Clamp each floor timber to the keel before boring commences there, and do the counterboring for the bolt head before boring for the shank. (Note in the photo that a shim was needed for a wood-to-wood fit at that station.)

102 An alignment stick clamped to the floor timber, so a helper can sight the drill, gets the hole bored at the desired angle and ensures that it comes through the floor timber's opposite edge rather than through one of its faces partway down.

103 In order for the square-edged garboard plank to fit against the keel, the keel has to be beveled. How much bevel depends on the angle, or deadrise, of the garboard; that angle is being lifted here by means of a small bevel gauge. Because the change in angle is gradual, there is no need to lift these angles at every station; every other or every third station will do.

104 That angle is recorded for convenience on the face of the keel as shown, adjacent to where it was lifted. (Notice that the centerboard trunk post has been cut off to its final height little below flush with the keel face. Notice also that the trunk has been relocated a bit from what these photos show, based on our experience with the prototype.)

105 After it has been bored for the keelbolts and marked for beveling, the keel timber can be removed from the boat.

106 The beveling angles are picked up from where you recorded them on the face of the keel and are used as shown for guiding the spokeshave or plane in working down the corners of the keel. Since the garboards are 1/2" thick, that should be the minimum width of the bevel for an adequate caulking seam. A guideline for beveling can be drawn through the points that were marked on the side of the keel earlier, while it was still on the boat. (This should be done using a short piece of 1/2" wood laid along each frame with its pointed end in contact with the side of the keel.) Now, while the keel is off the boat, is a good

26

time to pare away its other two corners, bringing the keel's outside face to the same width as the top of ballast keel and deadwood. Later, with the boat upright, you can be fussier with the shape here, perhaps doing some hollowing to produce a fair transition between the hull and the appendages below it.

107 Since there is a potential for seawater leakage between the bedlogs and keel, the joint there—including the projecting ends of the posts—is liberally coated with 3M 5200 before assembly.

108 While it is off the boat and easily accessible, the exposed face of the keel timber should be primed with red lead to keep it from checking. 3M 5200 is also spread on the faying surfaces of the keel: in way of the centerboard trunk bedlogs, the stern knee, and the stem scarf.

109 The keelbolts, having been made up or ordered to the correct length, can now be

driven. A ring of cotton wicking goes under each head so there will be no leakage. (Undersized temporary bolts should be used for securing the thicker half floors to the trunk bedlogs now, to be replaced later by ballast keel bolts of the correct diameter.)

110 At the stem scarf, the keel is marked with a batten for cutting to a fair curve—an extension of the curve of the stem.

111 A drawknife quickly cuts to the line.

112 Now, by shifting the overhead shore as necessary, the three bolt holes can be bored all the way through and, because the keel has been cut down to more or less its finished thickness at the scarf, the holes can be first counterbored to depth with confidence. Keep the joint pushed tightly together so that shavings don't get into the 3M 5200.

113 After bolting, the overhead shore can be taken away and the keel-to-stem scarf can be planed fair without interference. A stopwater, shown on the construction plan, is required at this scarf.

114 Aft, the transom must be marked to match the keel width, as shown, before that part of the keel can be bolted.

115 It's obvious here how much easier it is to cut away excess wood from the transom with the keel shoved up and out of the way. One edge of the masking tape represents the transom centerline. Note that the floor timber at the stern knee has been snipped off for drainage, like those next to the centerboard trunk mentioned earlier.

116 Here is the keel timber all bolted down. Note that the transom has been cut to its final bevel, using a plywood outside-face pattern shown on the drawing. (The outside face is what you see in the completed boat and is therefore the face that requires special control in shaping.) Battens are used as well while the transom bevel is being cut to make sure the planking will lie fair over frames, floors, and transom.

117 Lining off for the planking involves marking where you want the plank edges to fall on the frames and at the stem and the transom. Although the plank widths are indicated elsewhere in these instructions, here is the reasoning behind their location. For a planking job that looks good and makes economical use of planking material, you're after planks that taper gracefully from the 'midship station, where the hull's girth is greatest, toward the bow and stern. You want the planks to be as straight as possible, since curved boat boards are scarcer than straight ones; and you want the planks to be as narrow as is practical at the bilge, because there will be less backing out required and, therefore, less waste. Mark the frames and transom with the specified information, then mark the intermediate frames by means of a batten which passes through the marks and hits the stem and transom in a fair curve. Except for the sheerstrake, you don't need to duplicate the given measurements and plank lines precisely; just achieve lines that are fair. You should adhere to the widths for the varnished sheerstrake, however, since a deviation is so obvious and can give the boat an entirely different (and sometimes far less beautiful) appearance. As indicated on the drawings, there are 10 planks on each side of the boat.

118 Here the outboard edge of the garboard is being marked on the frames. Marking need only be done on one side of the boat (the side nearest the workbench), and a pair of planks made from that one so-called "pattern side" of the hull.

119 Spiling for the garboard, and most of the planks that follow it, is a well-known technique, and if you're familiar with how to do it, or if you prefer another method—there are several—skip these next few steps. What's happening here is that information describing the curved edge of the garboard is being transferred to a spiling batten, which is now tacked to the hull as a surrogate garboard and will later be flopped onto the planking stock and used as a kind of pattern from which the garboard can be sawn. Specifically, the distance between the edge of the spiling batten and the rabbet line at the edge of the backbone is being measured and recorded.

120 Here's a close-up view. The distance measured in the previous step shows as $1^3/_{16}$" marked on the batten's face. The location and direction of the width-measuring line is marked across its face as well, and the garboard plank's width at that point has been recorded as 4⅝". (Strictly speaking, the direction of the 1³⁄₁₆" measurement should have been drawn on the batten, as well as its fore-and-aft location. In this case, however, because the gap between batten and rabbet is small and the edges are nearly parallel, you can eyeball the measurement square with the batten's edge and save some time.)

121 The same principles apply at the garboard's sharply curving forward end. The "point" of the garboard is recorded by giving its direction and distance (in this case 9"), as shown.

122 With the spiling batten laid on a piece of planking stock in such a way as to avoid the worst knots and to generally work everything to best advantage, the transfer of measurements begins. You simply do things in reverse order so the resulting plank will fit the space you measured earlier.

123 Width measurements can be laid off by slipping the thin ruler under the batten and aligning it with the measuring line. The keel edge of the plank has to be drawn first, however, as a measuring reference, and this was done by tacking a fairing batten through the marked points and connecting them with a continuous pencil line.

124 Chances are you'll have to do a little trying and shaving for a good fit next to the keel, but because this boat's garboard has an easy bend, this should present no great problem. After you get a good fit, plane a caulking bevel that runs in about two-thirds of the plank's thickness and opens to about ¹⁄₁₆" at the plank's outer face. The other edge away from the keel should be left square, since it is customary (and necessary) to plane a caulking bevel on *only one* joining edge of each plank.

125 & 125a
The planking process continues, as with the garboard. As the more curved shape of the bilge is approached, flat planks will no longer bear in full contact on the frames and will require hollowing or "backing out." Thicker planking stock will be needed—up to $5/8$"—in order to hold close to the specified, uniform $1/2$" thickness of the finished skin. A finger-type template tool (as shown in Photo 125a) can be used to pick up the frame curvature at several locations along where a given plank is to fit, and serve as a guide for backing out—a process that is best done with a round-bottomed wooden plane. After hollowing the inside plank face, it will be helpful to plane away some of the outer surface to bring the plank edges to about $1/2$". After the several planks so shaped have been hung (that is, fitted and fastened into place), you can begin fairing the hull with a smoothing plane, first running fore-and-aft to take off the obvious ridges...

126
...then working diagonally across the hull. A grinder like the one used to rough-bevel the molds, can be used here—carefully! There will be more about smoothing the hull later.

MAKING AND FITTING THE SHEERSTRAKES

127
The sheerstrakes can enhance this boat, or they can really detract from its appearance if they're not shaped just right. It is well worth the effort to measure for and make the sheerstrakes carefully. The first step is to establish where you want the upper and lower edges to lie on the boat. This means getting a fair sheerline marked on the frames at close to the designed location, and setting off the plank widths from this line. (Remember that the designed sheerline as shown on the drawings and as indicated by the cross spalls is the height of sheer at the o*utside* corner of the plank, not the inside one. Thus, because of

the hull's flare, extra wood—often called "beveling wood"—will have to be figured into the shaping and positioning of the sheerstrakes.) So as to be absolutely certain of the shape, we made a trial sheerstrake out of cedar, clamped it in place on the hull, and noted the minor adjustments that would be needed on the "real ones" in order for them to fit perfectly.

Spiling for the Herreshoff-type sheerstrakes may surprise you with off-the-mark results if you continue with the same method that you used for the earlier planks. The sheerstrake's non-uniform cross-section causes it to take a different "lay" when bent around the curve of the hull, and more accuracy will result from using a two-layer spiling batten made by attaching a $^1/_4$ x $^3/_4$" strip to the regular batten's outer face, thus simulating the swelled-out portion of the sheerstrake. With some fussing ahead of time, you can saw out the mahogany sheerstrakes with assurance that they'll fit. Here is the second sheerstrake of the pair being rough-sawn; the first one, here being used as a pattern, was marked from the cedar "trial" sheerstrake with adjustments as mentioned above.

128 After rough sawing, the second plank can be brought to the exact shape of the first by means of a shaper. (Although the sheerstrakes are shown in this photo, the same technique can be used for the rest of the planking. See *Building the Catspaw Dinghy*, a WoodenBoat book, and a series of articles in *WoodenBoat* magazine Nos. 26, 27, and 28, for more on this efficient method of getting out planks.)

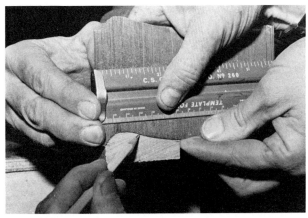

129 As a guide in sawing away the unwanted wood to form the sheerstrake "swell," a templating tool is used—the desired shape having been first lifted off an existing Herreshoff boat. The

correct shape is shown at full size on the drawing, and that shape can be transferred to the butt end of the sawn-out sheerstrakes in lieu of what's shown here.

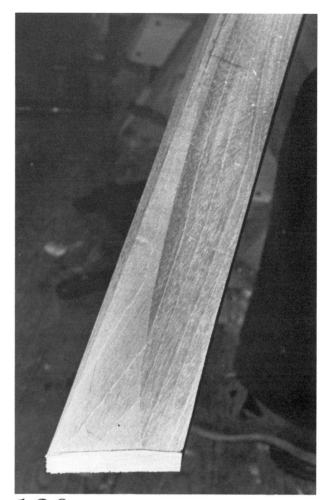

130a–g

Since the top edge of each sheerstrake is used as a reference (that is, as a starting point for the cross-sectional shape), that edge has to bear against the table saw's fence while the plank makes repeated passes over the blade, each pass being made with the blade at a different depth setting. The sheerstrake's reference edge, however, is concave in places, so to ensure that the saw makes its cut at a constant distance from it, you'll need a slightly crowned block screwed to the fence, as shown. After the sheerstrakes have been roughly "molded" by the saw, you can work in the rest of the shape with a chisel, a round-soled wooden plane, a scraper, a block plane, and coarse sandpaper—as shown in Photos 130a through f (left and previous page).

Photo 130g (above) shows the start of "dying out" the sheerstrake "swell" to bring the strakes forward and after ends to the same $1/2$" thickness as of the rest of the boat's planking.

Note: As an alternative to Steps 130 a–f, the sheerstrakes can be roughed out to their cross-sectional shape by passing them over the saw crosswise—or nearly so—rather than parallel to the blade.

33

131 We decided to fit and temporarily fasten on the sheerstrakes at this stage so they'd be precisely where we wanted them. None of the planks needed to be steamed, although the mahogany sheerstrakes were stiff and had to be securely clamped and fastened. In retrospect, I'd recommend steaming them on another boat.

132 The shape of the plank next to the sheerstrake could be traced from inside the boat after that plank was in position over the opening.

133 For ease in fitting, the traced planks were hung with the sheerstrakes removed.

134 Finally, the sheerstrakes are clamped into position and fastened. They have been brought to more or less their final cross-sectional shape, smoothed and varnished while they were off the boat. Rivets will be the final fastenings in certain areas of the sheerstrakes where the rivets will pass through frame heads or the sheer clamps. But the rivets will come later, after the hull is upright; for now, screws can be used.

135 The sheerstrakes taper at their forward and after ends to become a uniform ½" thick. Considerable tapering has been done here, although the plank's end has not yet been drawn into the stem rabbet.

136 It's time now for final smoothing; there are a variety of ways to go about it. A disc grinder is a good way to start, using 50 grit, assuming that the hull has already been planed roughly fair.

137 High places can sometimes be knocked down with course sandpaper stapled to a flexible board, as shown. A block of Styrofoam also works well. Keep feeling the surface; it has to be fair before there's much point in smoothing it.

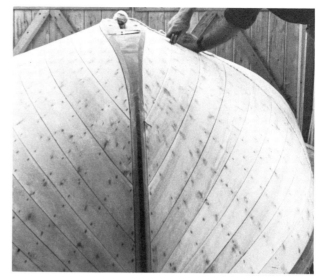

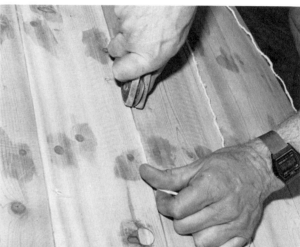

138a & b Screw holes are filled; we used epoxy resin and micro-balloons, a mixture that sticks well and sands easily. Caulking is best done with cotton wicking rolled in with a wheel.

139 Aft, the caulking strands are tucked into the plank seam, then split and worked into the hood-end seam at the transom.

140 The transom seam is then caulked with spun cotton driven not too hard into the seam and over the split wicking from the ends of the planks. Loose caulking can be driven further into the seams as is being done here. The garboard seam and the rabbeted seam at the stem are also caulked with spun cotton driven in with a small caulking iron and hammer or mallet. The seams, after caulking, should be primed with paint to saturate the cotton so it will stay put and be reasonably water-resistant.

141 Now for marking the painted waterline, an easy task while the hull is still upside down. Transverse straightedges, leveled as shown, should cross the hull at the height of the waterline—at the bow and the stern. A string should then be drawn tightly between the straightedges on each side of the hull. (Check that the string touches the fattest part of the hull the same distance from the sheer on each side.) The setup for marking is now complete, and the hull can be marked at intervals along both sides by one person while another sights across the string and tells him where to make the mark. The eye level of the sighter should always be at the waterline plane as determined when the string and one of the straightedges are aligned with the eye. The sighter has to keep mov-

ing to a new vantage point every so often in order to keep everything in view.

142 The waterline has been scribed by connecting the marks made in the previous step with a batten, then scraping or sawing a slight groove in the planking next to it. That gives you an easy line to paint to, which is being done here.

143 Prime painting should not only seal the wood, but should also saturate the caulking with paint (if not done as a separate operation earlier). Seam compound comes next.

144 The boottop line uses the scribed waterline as a reference and is located (by means of a level and a square) to be about $1\frac{1}{4}''$ above the waterline when viewed from the side. This means that the boottop's actual width on the hull will be greater because of the flare—an especially noticeable occurrence at the after end. Snazzier looks can be had by widening the boottop forward, starting 3' or 4' back from the stem and gradually increasing its height (measured vertically) to 2". Be very careful to get a fair line and an even taper because, like the sheerstrakes, the waterline is very obvious visually.

145 If you don't think the hull is as fair as it should be all over, now is the time to go after those bad places, using the technique described earlier, before the finish coats of paint are applied. The forward part of the hull is especially troublesome because of all the curves and contoured surfaces meeting there.

TURNOVER

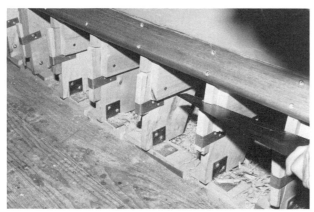

146 When there's no further advantage to the upside-down position, you can cut the hull free and turn it over. A word of caution, however: Don't cut away all the molds, but unscrew a few from the shop floor so they'll hoist away with the hull and ensure that the boat's shape doesn't change. A mold should be kept with the boat in way of each of the lifting slings, and there should be one amidships. But just as important, you should plan on keeping at least one mold—three would be better—in the flaring, forward part of the boat which, without this stiffening, would surely pinch together and create a hump in the sheerline.

147 The hull is hoisted vertically free of the molds (except for those mentioned earlier that go with the hull) and held there while the floor-mounted molds are removed. Then there'll be clearance for the hull to be turned upright in the slings.

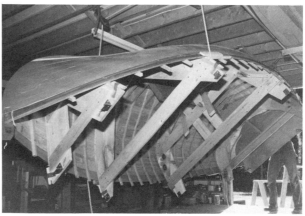

148 The hull can be easily rolled over in the slings if they're rigged as shown — that is, so the slings will "pass" or "run" through the overhead blocks. Chafe protection is needed at the sheer and at any other places where the sling may bear heavily on the planking.

THE SHEER CLAMPS

149 Of course, the first thing you'll want to do after the hull is upright is to get rid of the molds that were left in the hull. Since their purpose was to keep the hull from squeezing together or otherwise changing its shape, they should not be taken out until you've screwed several temporary 1 x 4" stretchers in place across the hull, as shown. Stretchers should be as high as possible (where they're most effective) and still allow space for the sheer clamps to be sprung in above them. *Take particular care that the hull doesn't pinch together forward,* or you risk spoiling the sheerline with a powderhorn shape. Keep checking that the boat's beam hasn't changed, and keep sighting the sheerline to make sure it stays eye-sweet. You can prime-paint the hull interior at this point after some sanding in the cockpit area, where the frames and planking will forever be visible. The frames here should be sanded or scraped to make their inboard faces slightly convex, and their sharp corners should be relieved to a "sandpaper round."

Now make up a deckbeam mold whose length is a little more than the boat's beam, with a curved edge sawn to the desired deckbeam crown (1¹/₂" in 5' for this boat). The beam mold will be put to a number of uses as the work progresses; here it will determine the bevel you'll be planing on the sheer clamp. Pick up the bevels as shown in the photo, using of a small bevel gauge to measure the angle between the underside of the beam mold and the face of the frame. Repeat this at about every third frame (note that the frames have been numbered for easy reference), and use a bevel board for recording the information.

150 The sheer clamps are of Douglas-fir, milled to 1³/₄ x 1⁵/₁₆", and long enough to run in one length from bow to stern. The beveling is all done on the outboard face, and like the frame-heel bevels shown earlier, the bevel here need only run across about two-thirds of the face width; as long as the sheer-clamp rivets will pass through the bevel, you're OK. Now, for a finished appearance, plane a ¹/₈" chamfer along the inboard lower corners of both sheer clamps.

151 The sheer clamps land against the tops of the frames, except way aft, where they seat in rabbeted oak blocks. Here, the starboard block is being fitted to the hull where it will soon be bedded and fastened; the rabbet has yet to be cut.

152 Here is that same block after rabbeting, ready for installation. 3M 5200 is being spread over the faying surfaces. Wood screws will secure the blocks to both transom and hull planking.

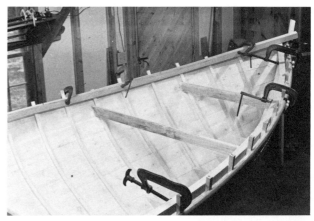

153 The sheer clamps are a little tricky to install, and their forward portions will definitely have to be steamed. I'd recommend positioning the steam-softened forward ends of the sheer clamps just about where you want them to ultimately rest (indicated by marks on the frames based on height and crown of deckbeams), starting at the stem and working back to about amidships, although, as the photo shows, we did otherwise. I'd further suggest two or three additional stretchers up forward fastened to the projecting frame heads above the sheerline to hold the hull shape there against the force of the sheer clamps as they're being drawn out against the hull. Notice on the drawings that the sheer clamps have a squiggle between frames number 7 and number 9 where they dip down as they run forward, so the deckbeams can rest on them. Back in the cockpit, where there are no beams, the clamp is at sheer level.

154 This photo shows what we did aft, but as I said earlier, this was probably not the best method. The curve here is comparatively gentle—and you can probably allow the clamps to run out past the corners of the transom and trim them off later. What this photo does point out, however, is how the two sheer clamps can be pushed apart or pulled together with shores or cords (as with the Spanish windlass pulling the ends of the clamps together here) so there is minimum stress on the hull. Note that the top of the transom has been cut to shape, something that's worth doing soon after the hull is upright so you don't get snagged by its sharp corners.

155 This is what the after end of the port sheer clamp should finally look like when seated into the oak quarter block. The blocks themselves will always be visible and should be smoothed and rounded a bit at their lower corners.

156 Aft of amidships, where the clamps are at sheer height, you can use the deckbeam mold for a guide in cutting off the frames and in establishing the correct up-and-down position of the sheer clamps. Copper rivets will fasten the sheer clamps, and will serve as the top row of sheerstrake fastenings as well. Angle the rivet holes alternately up and down so that the inboard ends will take on a zigzag pattern on the face of the sheer clamp and result in better holding. You'll be starting in the same counterbored holes you used to screw the sheerstrakes to the frames earlier, when the boat was still upside down; simply back out those temporary screws, one at a time, and re-bore all the way through for the rivets, as described above.

157 This shows the sheer clamp squiggle, spread over about four frames. The sheer clamp is braced for fastening; notice the zigzag riveting pattern.

158 The beveling wood has to be cut away from the top edges of the sheerstrakes and the sheer brought very close to its final line before the forward portions of the sheer clamps can be set to the correct height. The deckbeam mold, used in conjunction with your eye (keep sighting the sheerline), is the guide for this operation.

159 The forward frame heads can be cut down as well, to the sheer height and the beam-mold angle.

160 If the frame heads must be cut away still more, use a grinder (with a light touch) to avoid end-grain splintering.

161 Keep checking with the deckbeam mold until it lies fair, like this, everywhere across the hull. The sheer clamp rivets take on a different pattern in the forward part of the boat. They go through the *lower* edge of the sheerstrake, replacing that row of temporary screws. The top row of screws are temporary as well; they, too, are replaced by rivets which head up on the face of the frames.

162 As the final step in installing the sheer clamps, a mahogany breasthook is fitted over their forward ends where it secures the sheerstrakes and stem. Screws as well as 3M 5200 are used here, the screws being driven through the breasthook into the stem and the clamps, and through the sheerstrakes into the breasthook. Note the rivets at the sheer clamp and the frame head.

SOME DETAILS

163 Chamfering the frame heads makes things look better, and if you decide to use a block plane instead of a grinder to dress the frames to their final height, the chamfer will prevent most of the end-grain splintering.

164 The stemhead can also be cut to its designed height and angle.

165 When the shaping is complete, the stemhead, the sheerstrakes, and the top of the breasthook should look about like this. The upper part of the stem face will be notched later for the bronze chainplate that attaches to it.

166 The transom's edge gets a winding bevel that parallels the hull at the sheer when viewed from above, and becomes about halfway between being level and being square with the transom face when viewed from the side. The edge is planed to be slightly convex, and the sharp corners are rounded as shown. Take care here: the bevel changes character very quickly, and it's easy to pare away too much wood.

BEAMS AND BULKHEADS

167 The beams that will support the floorboards are of oak and are located on every frame, as shown in the plans. A measuring fid, used in conjunction with a fore-and-aft straightedge, determines the length and cut of each of the beams.

168 This is how the floorboard beams are fitted and fastened; they're notched over an inboard support piece at the centerboard trunk, and they land directly on the frames at their outboard ends.

169 It's easier to keep up with the painting as the boat is being built, because things are accessible. Note that separate beams are not needed aft of the trunk.

170 Beams that support the foredeck are also of oak and are sawn to the curve of the deck-beam mold shown earlier. Their ends are bolted through the sheer clamps and screw-fastened to the frameheads, those heads first being flattened a bit for a good fit against the beams. The aftermost deckbeam is thicker than the rest and is straight along its lower edge for extra face width near the center, where the mast partner casting will land. The ends of this beam may have to notch over the sheer clamp, as ours did. The watertight bulkhead has been started here: vertical stiffeners are in, and the planking is about half fitted. It lands against a hull frame and, as in similar situations mentioned elsewhere, the after side of that frame will need its corner flattened so the bulkhead planking has a decent landing. As shown on the drawings, this bulkhead is to be canvas covered (use the same method as described for the afterdeck) and serves as a watertight boundary between the cockpit and the flotation compartment forward of it. The foredeck, coamings, and any bolted-on hardware that requires access to this compartment should be in place before the bulkhead is completed, however.

171 At their lower ends the bulkhead stiffeners, except for the center one, will need to be notched over the frames, as shown.

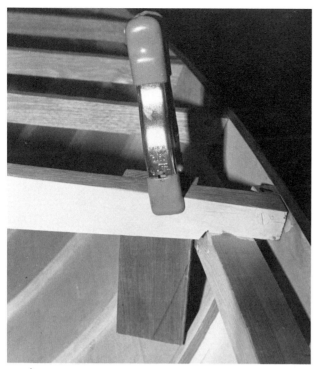

172 This photo shows how the frame has been dressed down to form a bit of a landing place, and how the corner block is fitted by scribing.

173 The afterdeck is below the sheer and therefore will need fore-and-aft risers to support the beam ends. Risers can be cedar, since the beam ends don't fasten into them. Instead, they are screwed to the hull frames, as shown. Notice that the floorboards within the underdeck storage compartment have been fitted and the area painted out beforehand when access was still good. The beams aft are flatter than those of the foredeck, although they still have a little crown—about 1" over their length.

174 The slotted sill piece sits on a floor timber and serves to support and retain the lower edge of the after bulkhead.

175 The after bulkhead itself is made of ½"-thick cedar boards, glued up for width. The bulkhead is made up in two separate halves for ease in fitting to the hull. The port half is shown here being scribed to fit.

176 This is the starboard half after it has been fitted and trimmed along its other edges. A vertical oak stiffener has been attached to the inboard edge to serve also as a jamb for the removable door to seat against. An oak support cleat for the cockpit seat is being positioned here and will be fastened with screws driven through the bulkhead from its after face into the oak.

177 All the beams are in place now, along with both halves of the bulkhead, and the transom-mounted support cleats upon which the decking will land. The removable center section of the compartment's floorboards rests on the beams while its paint dries.

AFTER DECKING

178 Because the afterdeck is bounded on three of its four sides, fitting a panel of plywood would take about as much time as individual cedar boards—and the cost of material would be a whole lot greater. Besides, cedar is always more fun to work with. This shows one of the deck planks being scribed to fit against the transom.

179 The bevel has to be picked up as well.

180 Finally, once the after end of each plank has been cut and fitted against the transom, the forward end can be marked for cutting, to be flush with the bulkhead face. Blocking for the boom crutch should be fitted between the beams as shown on the drawings before you lay the deck.

181 At the forward corners of the cockpit, a diagonal deck support like the one shown here should be made up and installed. Its curved shape can be determined by springing a batten along the inboard face of the sheer clamp and over the tops of the deckbeams, so that the batten lies just as the coaming eventually will. Remember that the outward-tipping coaming screw-fastens to the inboard face of this deck support; thus, this face must be beveled to match. Start with two chunks of oak that are plenty big—you'll be amazed how much shaping is required. The chainplates have been installed in this photo. They are backed up by oak blocks, as shown, with copper rivets through all.

COAMINGS AND FOREDECK

182 The steam-bent coamings come next, and you'll need a pattern to saw them out by. Use a thin, easily bent piece of wood (we used cedar), cut out a notch so that its forward portion can rest on the deckbeams, and spring it into place as shown. Scribe it, trim it, and/or mark it so it can serve as a proper pattern of the real thing. Be sure to allow a few inches of extra length at each end. As indicated on the drawings, the top of coaming should be 4" above the deck except from about the chainplates forward, where it gradually increases to measure (vertically) about 5" from the deck at its pointed end. Figure on a 1" overlap where it runs inside against the edge of the side deck and sheer clamp. (I know 1" doesn't sound like much, but there is really no need of more if you're careful to stagger the fastenings, one going into the covering board, the next into the clamp, etc.)

183 Here's a close-up of the coaming pattern as it runs by the diagonal deck support.

184 Only the bent forward ends of the coamings require steaming. This trap gives them some overbend to allow for springback after they cool and are unclamped. We allowed for about 2"; 5" or 6" of extra curve would have been better, especially with mahogany, since there was at least that much springback, which makes fitting the coamings into place a bit of a chore. Note the twist formed as a result of the trap's cross-pieces. Alternatively, the coamings can be bent right into the boat, fresh from the steam box and after the deck has been laid.

185 At this point, the trap-bent coamings can be laid aside until the deck is laid and sheathed. Mahogany plywood ³/₈" thick was used on the foredeck because it was easy to fit and because we wanted a stable surface for the canvas-and-epoxy sheathing we planned on using. The first task is to mark and cut out for the chainplates so the plywood will lie in full contact with the deckbeams and sheer-strakes for marking.

186 Notice that the raw edge of the plywood is cut back enough to center on the sheerstrake's top edge. A thin mahogany trim strip will be epoxy-glued along the outboard edge of the deck panels before they are installed in order to hide the plywood edge grain.

187 Some 3M 5200 laid along the top of the sheerstrake will ensure a strong, watertight connection to the foredeck panels. Screws, of course, are used here as well. Fastening elsewhere is by screws alone.

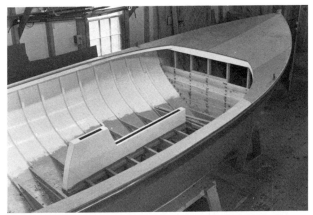

188 Both deck panels have been installed in this photo, as have the $7/16''$ solid mahogany covering boards aft of them which land on, bed

against, and fasten to the sheerstrakes and the sheer clamps. The plywood foredeck should be faired, smoothed, and filled in preparation for sheathing, and the covering boards should have a similar treatment (although its screw holes should be bunged) for a varnished finish. A short, $7/16''$-deep rabbet in the forward ends of the covering boards will give a flush landing surface for the foredeck sheathing.

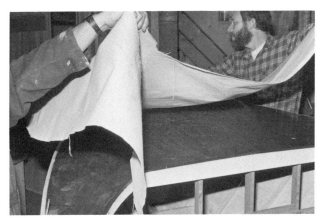

189 10-oz canvas, cut roughly to shape, is being laid in wet epoxy resin.

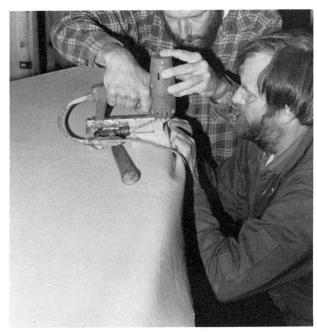

190 Monel staples hold down the edges after they have been pulled tight.

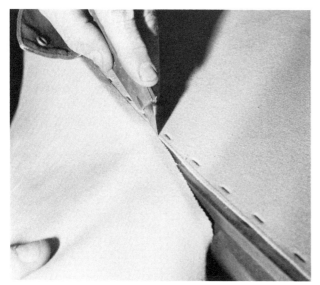

191 The canvas is cut back about ¹/₄" from the deck edge so it won't show under the toerail.

192 More epoxy is spread on top of the canvas to saturate and protect it.

193 We used canvas as well on the afterdeck, but laid it in white lead paste instead of in epoxy. The different covering systems were a bit of an

experiment to see if plywood and epoxy would outlast traditional cedar, canvas, and white lead. I imagine that the afterdeck will require recanvasing before the foredeck needs much of anything done to it. However, here it's an easy task, because nothing much sits on the afterdeck.

194 Canvas is laid in thinned-down white lead paste (thin it with linseed oil or turpentine to the consistency of very heavy cream), and pulled so it is free from wrinkles.

195 Monel staples are used at the forward and after edges.

196 The sheer clamps interfere with a stapler, or even a hammer, used in the usual way, along the sides of the deck. Copper tacks driven with the aid of a screwdriver work well here.

197 Another coating of white lead applied on top of the canvas fully saturates the fibers so they won't absorb water and rot—or, at least, that's the theory. We'll see what 10 years do to it!

198 Now, back to the coaming installation. Begin by notching the coamings' forward ends to lie on the foredeck. The notch's depth is about 1", and its location and underside shape can be lifted off the pattern as shown. The bevel can be picked up from the boat itself, being the angle between the aftermost deckbeam and the diagonal deck framing piece that the coaming will fay against. To discourage the notch from splitting, drive a 2"-long copper rivet or a piece of 1/8"-diameter bronze rod about where the "x" shows here on the coaming's lower edge.

198a Clamp the coaming against the sheer clamp as shown, letting the notch pretty much determine the coaming's fore-and-aft location. The coaming's after end, cut long, can be allowed to run uphill, to be fitted to the transom later. Scribe its forward portion down to the deck while a temporary centerline block fixes its rake, or outward cant. Reposition after scribing, and saw off the projecting end as shown so there will be room for the port coaming.

198b A temporary block should be plumbed and located with its edge on the boat's fore-and-aft centerline, as shown. Its forward face should be cut for the desired rake and bevel. Another block, a mirror image of this one, is used as an aid in fitting the port coaming. Both coamings are temporarily screwed to their respective blocks until they can be screwed to the deck from underneath. Then a single, permanent butt block as shown on the drawings is made to replace these. Be sure to seal and bed the coamings' end grain and give them an all-over coat of varnish before fastening them for good.

198c After their forward ends are fitted, the coamings' after ends can be measured and trimmed to fit against the transom at the correct height and the ogee endings cut as shown. Use a reference mark partway along the length of the coaming, say at station number 12, for reestablishing the fore-and-aft location of the coaming if it has to be removed for any reason before the fastening holes are bored. As to the fastenings, they are 1" No. 8 screws, except for the ones driven up through the deck, which should be about 1¼" long. All the fastenings should be bored for, then the coaming removed, its faying surfaces varnished to seal them against moisture (and the discoloration that goes with it), smeared with bedding compound, and reinstalled—this time, permanently. The coamings can then be dressed to their specified 4" height above the covering board, and marked for a gradual taper from station number 10 forward to the 5"-high pointed end. After dressing to that line, the top edge should be rounded as shown on the plan.

THE BALLAST KEEL AND DEADWOOD

199 The ballast keel mold should be made from pine boards as shown on the plans. Here it is ready for the melted lead. Note that the keel is poured bottom up, with its straight bottom being the open surface. You can just catch a glimpse of the on-edge board inserted to form the centerboard slot. The two pipes sticking up are vents to release the trapped gas from the closed forward section.

200 The mold was partially buried in the sand, and the melted lead poured into until just above the marks, to allow for shrinkage. In this picture, the lead has cooled, and the covered forward portion of the mold with the vent pipes has been removed. Be careful with hot lead, and wear eye, foot, and hand protection. Melt a little more than you think you'll need, as there is always some lost in the pouring proess.

201 The ballast keel casting is being smoothed and faired with a power plane prior to being placed under the boat. Note that the casting is on planks with pipe rolls under it for easy moving.

202 The ballast keel is about ready to roll under for a trial fit. The boat has been placed on sawhorses for easier access.

203 Another view. If the boat and keel had been on a smooth floor, things would have been

49

easier. The keel was rolled under the boat, and when the fit was good, the holes for the keelbolts were bored from the inside out. (Oak blocks were used in the centerboard slot to ensure alignment.) The keel was then removed, and counterbored for the bolt heads. It was then repositioned, the lengths of the bolts were measured, the top of the keel was covered with white lead and tarred felt, and the bolts were made and installed.

204 The oak fairing piece which fills the space forward of the ballast keel has been fitted and fastened here and is being faired off.

205 Five pieces of Douglas-fir have been roughed out and glued up to make the after deadwood.

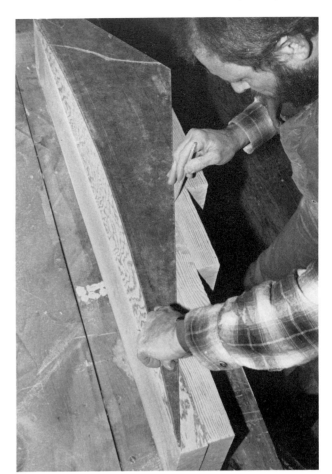

206 A pattern of the space to be filled has been made, and is being used to mark out the deadwood.

207 Another pattern of the plan view shape is used to mark the top of the deadwood. Note that the centerboard slot intrudes on the forward end of the deadwood.

208 It helps to have a good-sized bandsaw for sawing out the deadwood.

209 The deadwood has been fitted, bolt holes bored, and white lead spread on faying surfaces. The oak sternpost (not shown) will fill the remaining space aft of the deadwood.

210 Here she is with ballast keel and deadwood attached, faired, and painted. Before lowering the boat, the finished centerboard (see next section) was slipped up through the slot, a hole bored for its pivot pin, and the pin made and installed.

THE CENTERBOARD

211 Two layers of $\frac{1}{2}$" mahogany plywood are glued together to form the centerboard. Make sure it's firmly clamped for gluing, especially at the edges, and that there is no warping. Three sides should be rounded (I ran a router around the edges of the pieces before gluing them together), and the trailing edge—the edge nearest the camera— should be more gradually tapered thin, as shown on the plan. Later, after the glue cures, a 5 x 8" cutout will be made in the lower, after part of the board (as shown on the drawing), and poured full of ballast lead.

THE RUDDER

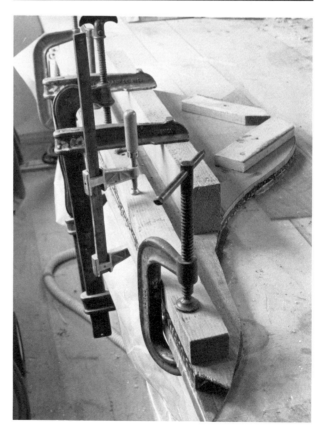

212 The rudder is glued up about like the centerboard, except that its thickness should total

1⅛". It, too, is to be tapered on its after edge for less drag through the water. Installation of check pieces at the top and cast-bronze pintles along the leading edge complete the job.

THE SPARS AND RIGGING

213 The spars consist of a mast, a boom, and a jib club; if the boat is to be the gaff-rigged version, a gaff will be required as well. All are solid and round, so making them is a very straightforward operation. Dimensions are shown on the plans, and any good book on boatbuilding will show what techniques to use in laying them out, cutting the tapers, and converting them from square to round. The mast can be glued up in halves if the full-dimension stock isn't available. Gaff jaw detail is also shown on the drawing, and the finished product shows in this photo.

214 To hold the spliced loops of the standing rigging in place, wooden "hounds" will be needed to uphold the Herreshoff tradition. These can be made from any convenient softwood hollowed out in a single length, as shown.

215 After rough cutting and shaping, the pieces can be glued in place on the mast—three pieces (to go about halfway around) are needed for each hound. The forestay hound should be placed highest on the mast, with the shroud hounds below it. A length of shock cord, stretched and wrapped around each set of hounds as shown, will hold them snugly to the mast while the glue cures, after which the finished shaping can be accomplished.

216 The wire standing rigging, spliced around the mast, consists of a pair of shrouds and a forestay. If a gaff is used, bridle of rope or wire will be needed for the peak halyard block to ride on. Running rigging is best made of 5/16" three-strand Dacron, although the the mainsheet will be easier to handle if it is a little larger in diameter—say, 3/8" or 7/16".

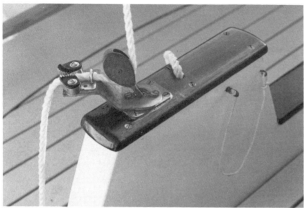

217 The centerboard trunk, showing main-sheet lead block and cam cleat mounted on a swivel base. The rope centerboard pennant shows as well, coming through a bored hole in the trunk cap. A bronze pin, connected to the trunk by a lanyard so it won't get lost, holds the centerboard in the fully raised position.

218 The bronze angle, which is detailed on the plans, connects the coamings to the transom. Wood screws into the transom and lower edge of the coaming, and machine screws through the top part of the coaming and into the tapped holes of the casting provide secure fastening.

219 This is the butt block at the coamings' forward end.

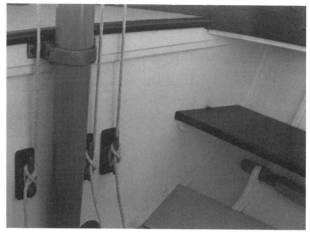

220 Mast bail, halyard cleats, oar holder, and seat support.

221 The rudderhead and the tapered after end of the tiller.

222 The forward end of the tiller, showing the familiar Herreshoff egg-shaped knob.

223 The forward end of the jib club is hooked to the stem as shown.

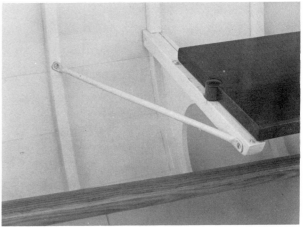

224 The removable seats join over a braced and bracketed support, and lock over a wooden pin as indicated on the drawings. The red-cedar seat option would provide storage for four PFDs.

Use and Care

Afloat, your Haven 12½ will have a decidedly big-boat feel. The stability and momentum that come from her lead ballast keel are not to be found in the usual 16-footer, and her large, spacious cockpit would more likely go with a 25' or 30' boat. If you've sailed small craft, however, you'll feel right at home—downright comfortable, in fact—in the Haven 12½. Here are a few pointers that will add to the joy of using her:

(1) Set up the shrouds just tight enough to keep the mast from whipping as the boat dances on her mooring.

(2) Raise and pin the centerboard while the boat is moored.

(3) In getting underway, hoist the mainsail before the jib, and on the gaff-rigged model take up on the peak halyard until diagonal wrinkles appear, running from peak to tack. The marconi mainsail's halyard should be pulled as tight as you can get it before cleating. The jib halyard should be just tight enough to cause the forestay to go a bit slack. In lowering the sails, drop the jib before the mainsail; it's an indication of good seamanship and helps prevent the boat's bow from blowing off downwind after you've picked up the mooring.

(4) Close-hauled, these boats sail better if allowed to "foot" rather than "point." This is especially true in a chop with very light air, so don't overtrim the sails when you're trying to sail to windward.

(5) Be prepared to quickly slack the mainsheet in puffy winds; the Haven 12½ can be accidentally—and suddenly—heeled enough to take solid water over the lee rail. Unless relieved of wind presure, the boat will

remain excessively heeled until its cockpit is completely filled with water. Although you need not fear an out-and-out sinking (because of the watertight compartment formed by the bulkhead and foredeck), you risk loss of gear, considerable embarrassment, and a through soaking.

(6) Keep the boat in correct fore-and-aft trim. Too many people sitting on the afterdeck depresses the stern and drastically reduces boat speed.

(7) Moored boats should be kept free of bilgewater. Consider fitting a boom tent to shed rainwater during long, unattended periods. Open the forward compartment's deck plate vent for air circulation when the boat isn't being sailed.

(8) Use the main halyard (on the marconi model) to back up the boom crutch and avoid damage from a scraping, flailing boom when you're not around to secure it. Simply pass the halyard's end (cast off from the sail) around the boom just aft of the aftermost sheet block, and tie it back on itself, then take up on the other end (the hauling part) until it is tight and make fast as usual to the bulkhead-mounted halyard cleat. The peak halyard, if pulled tight with the sail furled, will supplement the boom crutch on gaff-rigged boats.

Good care is *consistent* care. It means doing what is needed *when* it is needed. Here are a few suggestions:

(1) Paint (and varnish) the entire boat annually, except perhaps the hull interior (planks, frames, and bulkheads) where the wear is minimal and excessive paint film buildup is difficult to sand or strip. Before re-coating, sand sufficiently to remove unwanted buildup as well as to fair and smooth the surface. (Remember, however, that a reasonably thick paint film (say, four to six coats) greatly stabilizes the wood against shrinking and swelling, and that this applies to the inside of the boat as well as the outside.) Newly built hulls will need a season afloat to "settle in," after which the squeezed-out seam compound can be faired and smoothed—and be expected to stay that way. We strongly recommend traditional oil-based paints and varnishes as being the most appropriate finishes for this traditional boat: they're easy to use, low in cost (compared to "space-age" finishes), and proven in durability.

(2) Boats in storage should rest on their keels, not on their bilges.

(3) If there is even a remote chance of water collecting in your stored boat, bore a $\frac{5}{8}$" or $\frac{3}{4}$" hole through the garboard in the low point of the bilge. A simple, tapered, softwood plug through the hole can serve thereafter. Open the forward compartment vent plates while the boat is in storage.

(4) Inside storage in a damp, unheated shed is highly recommended. Alternatively, use a pitched, canvas cover over the entire boat, including the topsides. Plastic covers can't "breathe" like woven canvas can, and are not recommended. Outdoor storage should be in the shade and close to damp ground, the objective being to retard, minimize, or perhaps altogether avoid the opening up of hull seams through drying out of the planking.

Table of Plank Widths

Frame No.		3	8	13	18	Stern
Garboard	1	$7/_8$	$5^1/_4$	$5^3/_4$	5	$2^1/_4$
Broadstrake	2	$5^1/_8$	$5^1/_4$	$5^3/_8$	$5^1/_4$	$5^1/_4$
	3	$4^1/_2$	$4^7/_8$	$5^1/_4$	$5^1/_8$	$4^3/_4$
	4	$3^1/_2$	$4^5/_8$	$5^1/_4$	$4^{15}/_{16}$	$4^3/_8$
	5	$3^1/_4$	$4^1/_4$	$4^1/_2$	$4^1/_4$	$3^3/_8$
	6	$2^7/_8$	$3^{13}/_{16}$	$4^3/_8$	$3^{11}/_{16}$	$2^1/_2$
	7	$2^7/_8$	$3^7/_8$	$4^1/_4$	$3^5/_8$	$2^7/_8$
	8	$3^5/_{16}$	$4^1/_2$	$4^5/_8$	$3^7/_8$	$2^7/_{16}$
	9	$3^9/_{16}$	4	$4^5/_8$	$3^7/_8$	$2^1/_2$
Sheerstrake	10	$2^3/_4$	3	$3^1/_8$	$3^1/_8$	$2^1/_4$

Schedule of Major Fastenings

Stem and keel scarfs .... $5/16$" bronze carriage bolts

Floors to frames .... #10 copper rivets

Floors to keel .... $5/16$" bronze carriage bolts

Transom drifts .... $1/4$" bronze rod

Stern knee to transom .... $1^3/4$" #12 FHWS*–bronze

Planking to frames .... 1" #8 FHWS–bronze

Sheerstrake (top edge) to frames 1-7 .... #10 copper rivets

Sheerstrake (lower edge) to sheer clamp(frames 1-7) .... #8 copper rivets

Sheerstrake (top edge) to sheer clamp (frames 8-22) .... #8 copper rivets

Centerboard trunk sides to posts and bedlogs .... $1^1/4$" #10 FHWS–bronze

Deckbeams to sheer clamps (foredeck) .... 3" #10-32 FHWS–bronze

Deckbeams to frame heads .... $1^1/4$" #8 FHWS–bronze

Decking—forward and aft .... 1" #8 FHWS–bronze

Coamings .... 1" #8 FHWS–bronze
($1^1/4$" #8 up through foredeck)

Floorboards and margin .... 1" #8 FHWS–bronze

Ballast keel to hull .... $7/16$" bronze bolts

After deadwood to hull .... $3/8$" bronze bolts

Rudder cheeks .... #8 copper rivets

Rudder gudgeons .... $1^1/2$" #14 FHWS–bronze

* FHWS = flathead wood screws

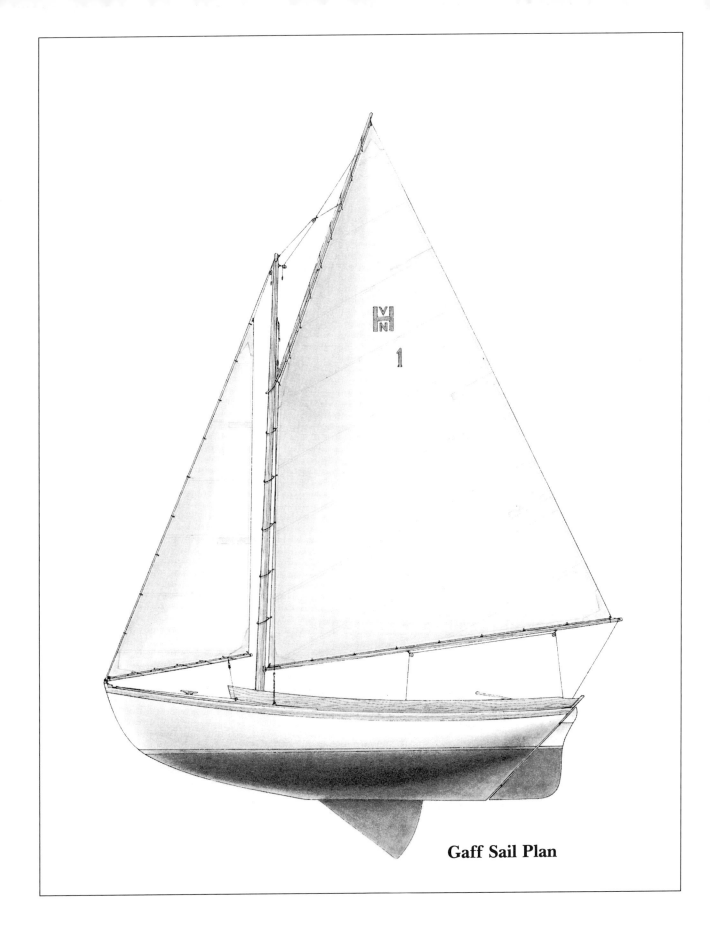

Gaff Sail Plan

Marconi Sail Plan

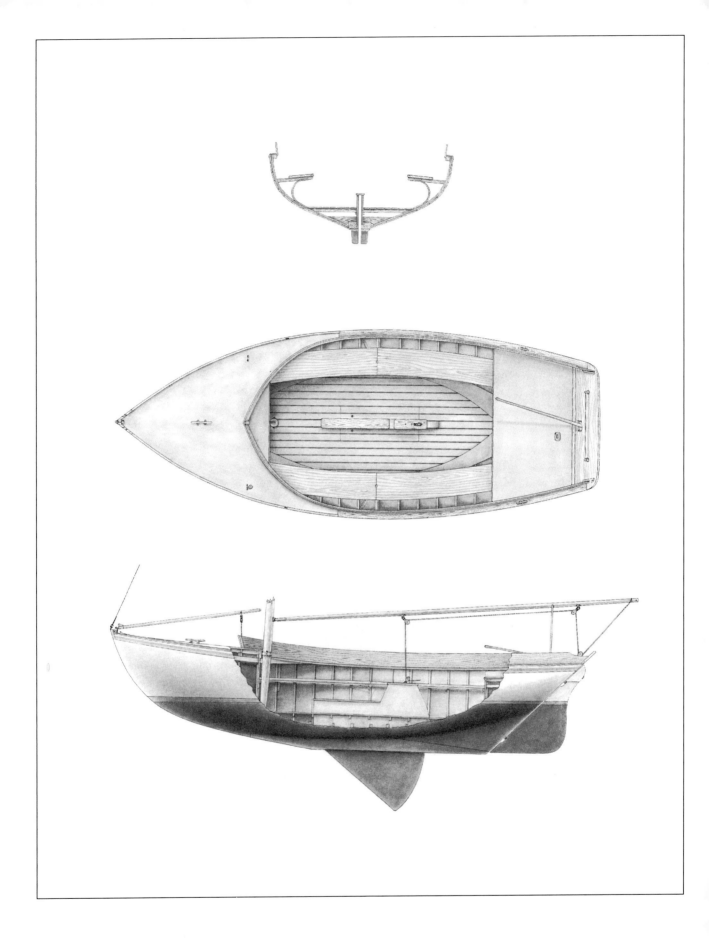

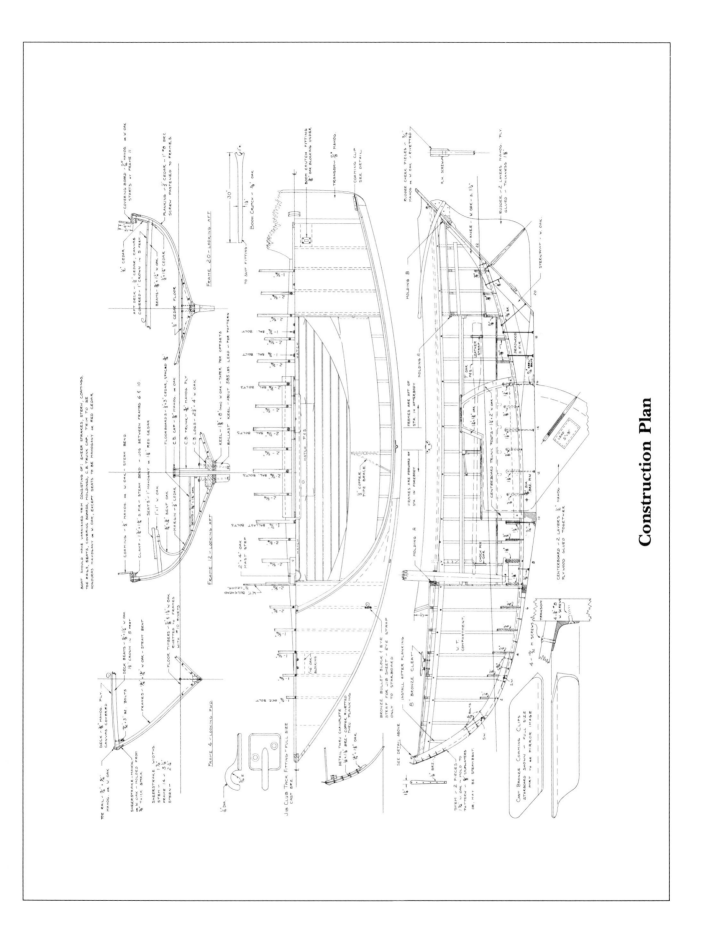

Construction Plan

61

Spars, Hardware, and Bulkheads Plan

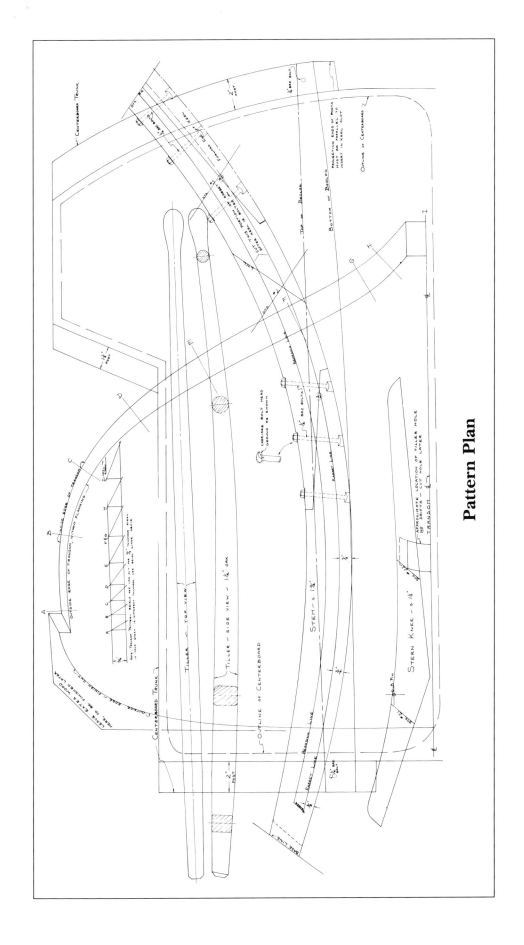

Pattern Plan

63